CW00404440

J'AIME PARIS

ALAIN DUCASSE

hardie grant books
MELBOURNE · LONDON

PARIS

has been around for a long time! Steeped in a history with close ties to its great culinary tradition, it is known for its fashions and whims, as well as its authentic creations. It is a place where the art of entertaining and the science of gastronomy are actively encouraged by a public of discriminating tastes. Yet it is more than just the grand establishments of haute cuisine, the charming bistros and brasseries of yesteryear - Paris is the setting for new sensations and innovation. Paris breathes an atmosphere that inspires excellence, inventiveness and renewal. I love both the left and right banks of the city. I love Paris for its unpredictable diversity; it never ceases to surprise me. If only there were more hours in the day, it would be such a pleasure to stroll, shop and dine whenever the urge took me, in the miniature cities known as the quartiers. Paris is far from my origins in the south, but the everchanging scenery, which invites you to go on imaginary journeys through time and space, makes it feel like home.

— HOW TO USE THIS GUIDE —

Discover one hundred essential Paris addresses in eight chapters, covering different zones, each with its own unique tourist appeal. Each one - reflecting a particular side to this city that is in constant flux between trend and tradition - is a genuine landmark for food lovers. Locate them easily using the maps provided at the beginning of each chapter, where you'll find each establishment marked with its corresponding page number.

Depending on where your walks take you, break for a legendary morning croissant by the Canal Saint Martin, make a pit stop at the terrace of a café, check out local markets with enticing, brightly coloured stalls, find delight in fine dishes by the greatest chefs in the most magical places... There are countless possibilities, and they cater to every taste and budget. An icon next to each address quickly indicates the type of establishment you can expect to find (see key on the next page), and the price range located opposite will enable you to work out how much you will have to spend, before you step through the door...

Under 20€

20€-50€

50€-100€

100€-250€

More than 250€

— LEGEND —

 café

 bakery

 restaurant

 patisserie

 bar

 ice cream parlour

 coffee shop

 delicatessen

 confectioner

 chocolate factory

 butchery

 butcher

 hotel

 wine merchants

 brasserie

 kitchen supplies

 cheese monger

 tea

 market

 fish monger

CONTENTS

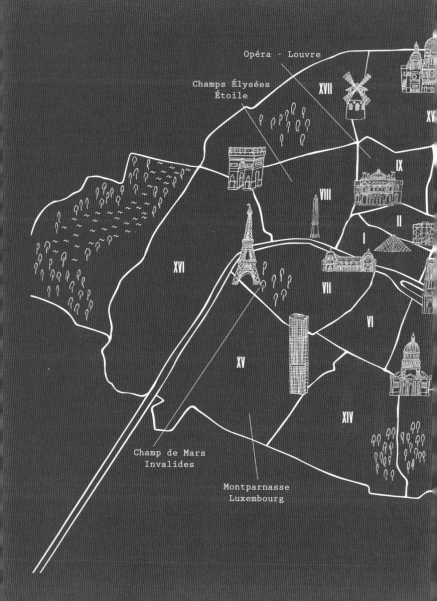

Opéra - Louvre

Champs Élysées
Étoile

XVII

XV

IX

VIII

II

I

XVI

VII

VI

XV

XIV

Champ de Mars
Invalides

Montparnasse
Luxembourg

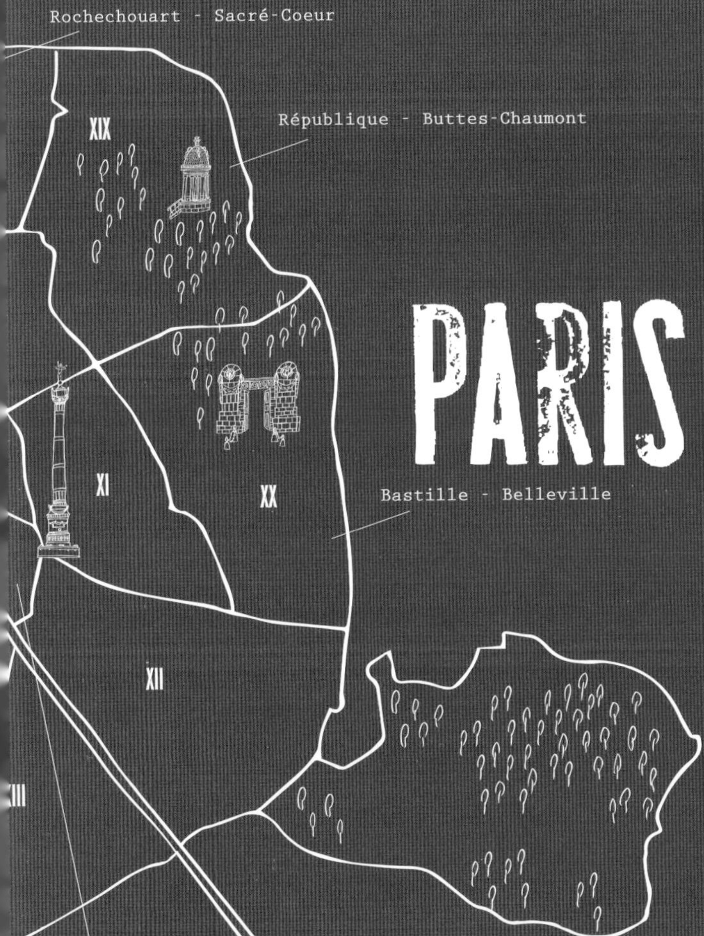

PARIS

Rochechouart - Sacré-Coeur

République - Buttes-Chaumont

Bastille - Belleville

Quartier Latin
Hôtel de ville

XIX

XI

XX

XII

III

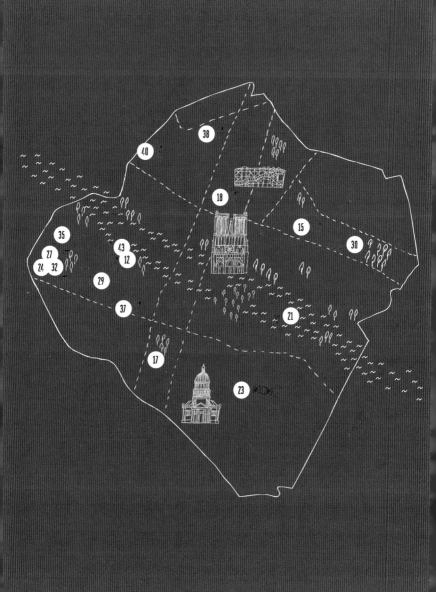

QUARTIER LATIN
LATIN

—

HÔTEL DE VILLE

ALLARD

The spirit of 'mother's cooking' lingers on in this kitchen. Proof of this are the frog's legs in the style of Fernande Allard, richly buttered and with a delicate hint of parsley, or the duck with olives, which comes golden and tender - done to perfection.

Here in the heart of the Saint-Germain-des-Prés neighbourhood, Allard refines his timeless skills, seasoned with his Parisian wit, for lovers of authenticity and good food. The *pâté en croûte* vies for attention with the poached eggs in wine, as does the beef cheek with the Bresse chicken. It's a real treat to feast on these dishes so lovingly prepared by Laetitia Rouabah, while you relax on your banquette and luxuriate in the delightful atmosphere of yesteryear.

 **— www.restaurant-allard.fr**

↑ **Allard** 41 rue Saint-André des Arts, Paris VIᵉ – P. +33 1 58 00 23 42

FRAICHES

s   Les 100

L'AS DU FALAFEL

Are they giving their falafels away? You'd almost think so, considering the queue that forms when it's close to eating time. Polite customers abound, even with staff seemingly detached from this world. Not a very exotic look - judging by the red canteen tray - but for nothing in this world would we go anywhere else. The crispness of their herb balls creates, for a minute, the illusion that we all have an Israeli grandmother. With a glass of lemonade - incredibly sweet, incredibly acidic - we're on holiday.

↑ **L'as du falafel** 32-34 rue des Rosiers, Paris IV[e] – P. +33 1 48 87 63 60

BALZAR

The terrace seems to have been set up for Smurfs! With your knees firmly wedged under your chin, you wonder if there might be other, less cramped, tables around the Sorbonne. But you go there for Sartre and Camus, or to wait until it's time for the cinema - where your seats will be even worse - and to be teased by the waiters. You also go there to enjoy such classic bistro fare as celery remoulade and leeks vinaigrette. It's an institution.

 — www.brasseriebalzar.com

↑ **Balzar** 49 rue des Écoles, Paris Vᵉ – P. +33 1 43 54 13 67

BENOIT

A landmark to the Parisian appetite for indulgence, Benoit has been treating the tastebuds of the French capital since 1912. But with a modern twist – true Parisian cuisine. Depending on the season, enjoy stuffed tomatoes or asparagus in mousseline sauce, followed by *sole à la Nantua* or Lucullus-style veal tongue. Then there is the rare pleasure of authentic profiteroles. You don't need an accordion player; the bistro's spirit sings on your plate.

— www.benoit-paris.com

↑ **Benoit** 20 rue Saint-Martin, Paris IVᵉ – P. +33 1 58 00 22 05

P. +33 1 43 54 31 61

29-31 rue Saint-Louis en l'île, Paris IVᵉ

Glacier Berthillon

GLACIER BERTHILLON

A biting-cold winter has hit Paris. In an empty tearoom, the entire Berthillon team, huddled together as if round a fireplace, is carefully crumbling a glistening mountain of candied chestnuts. Who eats ice-cream in this weather? The Parisians, it seems. They patiently await their turn, captivated by candied chestnut with a Christmas Eve scent. In summer, the chestnut gives way to wild strawberries, and the Parisians are joined by gourmets from around the world. We can understand why!

— www.berthillon.fr

LE BONBON AU PALAIS

The taste of a memory nestles in gleaming glass jars. The sweet slips from the tongue at the Palace - a *Sucre de pomme*, a multicoloured *Froufrou*, a *Negus*, a caramelised nut - and childhood sets off on its magic carpet ride. Each jeweller's marvel comes from the artisan who created it, sometimes a few centuries ago, sometimes according to a secret recipe still fiercely guarded by protective nuns.

— www.bonbonsaupalais.fr

↑ **Le bonbon au palais**   19 rue Monge, Paris Vᵉ – P. +33 1 78 56 15 72

BRASSERIE LIPP

This establishment is an historical monument. The 1900s interior
and façade are listed and even the menu has not changed in half
a century. But don't be put off by this. Whatever the season, you
must try the *choucroute* on your first visit. Like the unchanging
plant motifs on the tiled walls, you will still be offered the
choice of *blanquette de veau* (veal stew) or *boeuf gros sel* (boiled
beef). Like some of the regulars, the *millefeuilles* are substantial.

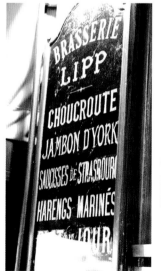

↑ **Brasserie Lipp** 151 boulevard Saint-Germain, Paris VIe – P. +33 1 45 48 53 91

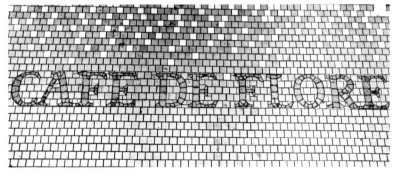

CAFÉ DE FLORE

The dish arrives boiling hot and golden. The regular customer barely looks at his Welsh rarebit, a melted Cheddar treat. It consists of tasty morsels of bread under a creamy, beer-flavoured coating *au gratin*. On the terrace, in the shadow of Sartre and his 'Beaver', you trace the back of your spoon over the green writing on the saucer while enjoying life. A cappuccino with the froth rising like a soufflé and a buttered slice of Parisian baguette are just the thing to start the day.

 — www.cafedeflore.fr

↑ **Café de Flore** 172 boulevard Saint-Germain, Paris VIe – P. +33 1 45 48 55 26

DA ROSA ÉPICERIE FINE

The roughness of natural stone walls. The rasping of a Portuguese accent burning up in the summer, icy in winter. The pungent and intoxicating aromas of Iberian hams curing along the ceiling. But, under the surface, the complex fruitiness of the bellota, which lasts in the mouth as long as a juicy tomato on some hot bread, the pepperiness of a cheese. In this deli-canteen that looks like none other, we settle in, as if in the Mediterranean...

 — www.darosa.fr

↑ Da rosa épicerie fine 62 rue de Seine, Paris VIᵉ – P. +33 1 40 51 00 09

DAMMANN FRÈRES

In the shade of the archways of the elegant Place des Vosges, the Dammann Frères tea house is a haven of peace. From selecting to importing teas, as well as creating new blends, this family business has been perpetuating its know-how for the past three generations. Besides original teas sold loose, in sachets or in balls, cold-infused teas and herbal infusions make you forget the goings-on in the Marais quarter and beckon you to distant travels.

 — www.dammann.fr

↑ Dammann Frères   15 place des Vosges, Paris IIIe – P. +33 1 44 54 04 88

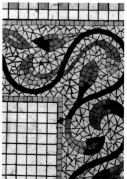

LES DEUX MAGOTS

The place to come to for the view and the cultural history of this district, which was partly written on these tables. Facing the Saint Germain church and the square where the Picasso statue stands, Les Deux Magots is one of the oldest Parisian cafés. It has always welcomed the inhabitants of Saint-Germain-des-Prés, celebrities and tourists, and has awarded a literary prize since 1933. Inside, certain drinks are still served by presenting customers with the bottle first. You must try a hot chocolate served the old-fashioned way.

 — www.lesdeuxmagots.fr

➜ **Les Deux Magots** 6 place Saint-Germain-des-Prés, Paris VIe
P. +33 1 45 48 55 25

LADURÉE

The Ladurée house remains true to its name. For almost 500 years, 16 rue Royale - one of the capital's very first tearooms - has been welcoming gourmets, regulars and tourists. In the heart of Saint-Germain-des-Prés, a special mention goes to the boutique on rue Bonaparte. Capturing the art of living the French way, Ladurée perpetuates the great patisserie tradition, while at the same time innovating through the blackcurrant-violet macaroon and the divine rose éclair.

 — www.laduree.com

↑ **Ladurée**   21 rue Bonaparte, Paris VIᵉ – P. +33 1 44 07 64 87

OENOSTERIA

A little piece of heaven in the guise of a corner of Tuscany. In this delicatessen extension of the nearby Casa Bini, delicious cold meats vie for your attention with a fine selection of ripe cheeses. If you're hungry, Fabiana can also offer you *gnudi* (nude) dumplings or *strozzapreti* (priest-stranglers) - so-called because this is the pasta of the poor, made without egg and served to priests when they came to visit their flock - accompanied by wines chosen with great care. And for dessert, you can try a classic tiramisu that is as light as a cloud.

↑ **Oenosteria** 40 rue Grégoire de Tours, Paris VIᵉ – P. +33 1 77 15 94 13

 — www.restaurant-oenosteria-paris.fr

PHARAMOND

The Caen-style tripe casserole has written the history of this establishment. Under the retro tiles and the copper mirrors, the lavish Norman veal rib appeals to mindless gluttony. Regulars gorge on magnificent escargots, stuffed with butter and garlic, and roasted to perfection. Guests of a higher standing enjoy the private rooms on the first floor, where the ghost of Clemenceau crosses paths with the ghost of Coluche. That could be interesting...

— www.pharamond.fr

↑ **Pharamond**   24 rue de la Grande Truanderie, Paris Ier – P. +33 1 40 28 45 18

YAM'TCHA

Potatoes? Just like that, in the wok, 45 sec-
onds, almost raw? The high priestess of the
flame officiates, and the spud, prepared like
green mango, is ennobled. Also transformed:
steamed aubergines enhanced with fermented
black beans, wedge clams in the wok, duck
in all its guises. Sit at the bar for a
bird's-eye view over the clever and skilful
work of Adeline Grattard.

— www.yamtcha.com

→ **Yam'tcha** 4 rue Sauval, Paris Ier – P. +33 1 40 26 08 07

ZE KITCHEN GALERIE

"My definition of cuisine is freedom of expression. I function between different desires, moods, passions, discoveries, travels. My inquisitiveness is the source of the cuisine I prepare today. I am also privileged to work with fabulous market gardeners - Joël Thiébault and Asafumi Yamashita - my goldsmith market gardeners, each of whom, with their own sensibility, brings me vegetables of incredible freshness and taste. I get on well with them; in fact, they're just like me, they feel and explore..."
William Ledeuil

 — www.zekitchengalerie.fr

↑ **Ze Kitchen Galerie** 4 rue des Grands Augustins, Paris VIᵉ – P. +33 1 44 32 00 32

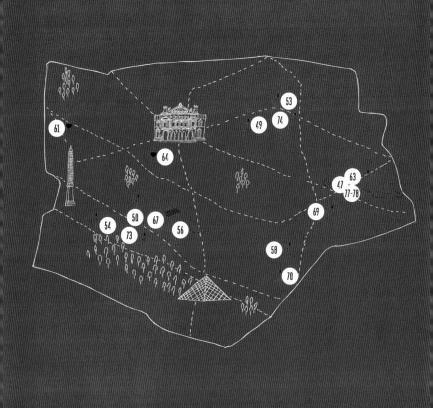

OPÉRA

—

LOUVRE

L'ARBRE À CAFÉ

In this little shop located in the middle of the rue du Nil you won't need coaxing to sample the exceptional coffees that Hippolyte Courty discovers around the world, and which he roasts himself here in Paris. There are so many top class varieties to be appreciated just as they are for their unique qualities - they sell themselves. Intense and authentic, they each tell a different story - of their lands of origin and of the people who grow them. These coffees, so full of vitality, will win over the uncertain.

— www.larbreacafe.com

↑ L'arbre à Café   10 rue du Nil, Paris IIe – P. +33 1 84 17 24 17

AUX LYONNAIS

There was once a typical Lyonnais *bouchon* (bistro) in the heart of Paris. There was no need to change anything, only to perpetuate its traditions. Each of the specialities prepared by Frédéric Thévenet, from the *pot de la cuisinière Lyonnais* to the *île flottante* and pink praline tart. There is also a second, less-heralded legacy. There was once a young chef, Alain Ducasse, he grew fond of the noble region of Lyon and its iconic chefs Paul Bocuse and Michel Troigros. Aux Lyonnais is a bouchon deserving of praise.

 — www.auxlyonnais.com

↑ **Aux Lyonnais** 32 rue Saint-Marc, Paris IIᵉ – P. +33 1 58 00 22 16

LE CARRÉ DES FEUILLANTS

At the end of a passageway, a box-like building stands on the site of the former Feuillant monastery built in the time of Henri IV. Alain Dutournier has a keen sense of beauty, and he treats us to elegant and contemporary dishes influenced by the food of south-west France. People come here to sample its generous, character-ful cuisine: foie gras, langoustines with sweet garlic nougatine, veal sweetbreads with fresh morels, and wild strawberry, rose and lychee macaroons. Place Vendôme is nearby, yet we could almost be in the south.

 — www.carredesfeuillants.fr

↑ **Le Carré des Feuillants** 14 rue de Castiglione, Paris Ier – P. +33 1 42 86 82 82

RESTAURANT CHARTIER

This reasonably priced restaurant has always had bouillon as its signature dish, a broth made from meat and vegetables served directly at the table. Chartier is popular for its unusual mix of simple bistro cooking and opulent theatrical décor. As if seated in a velvet-lined box, you can appreciate this quality simply by biting into an egg with mayonnaise. Canteen-style dishes are the order of the day, with grated carrots and cucumbers in cream. The menu scrawled on the paper tablecloth is almost worth framing.

— www.restaurant-chartier.com

↑ Restaurant Chartier 7 rue du Faubourg Montmartre, Paris IXe
P. +33 1 47 70 86 29

CHEZ FLOTTES

Monsieur Gérard brandishes his big knife, the plump loaf pressed against his body. He slices the fresh Poilâne bread by hand. "The secret is to slice it thinner than usual to enhance the flavour of the products. If you don't, you have nothing but bread in your mouth." During his time feeding nocturnal Parisians, Gilbert Flottes, together with Lionel Poilâne, invented a simple but tasty gem: the Poilâne croque-monsieur. Today, his son Olivier manages the family brasserie.

 — www.brasserie-flottes.com

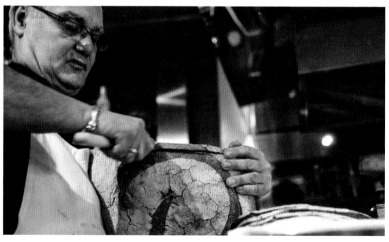

↑ **Chez Flottes** 2 rue Cambon, Paris Iᵉʳ – P. +33 1 42 60 80 89

L'ÉCUME SAINT HONORÉ

You can hear the cry of seagulls in the distance. There is a notice on the blackboard: 'For dessert, raw scallops, soy sauce! Tender, tasty!' Opened and cut in front of you, the beauty reveals itself to be sweet and flowery, the ideal dessert to round off an outstanding tasting. Because here, the large selection of oysters, clams, mussels and shrimp comes with freshness and optimum flavour.

FILETS DE ROUGET-BARBET 5€.70 (100g.)

Filets de 1kg 3 4.

Gourmet **LOBSTER**

SERVED DAILY ON THE BEACH
Always Fresh

L'ÉCUME ST-HONORÉ
BAR A HUITRES
OYSTER BAR
SALLE CHAUFFÉE
01.42.61.93.87

↑ **L'écume Saint Honoré** 6 rue du Marché Saint-Honoré, Paris Ier
P. +33 1 42 61 93 87

LES FINES GUEULES

You allow yourself to be recommended a good wine to go with a sausage you are having at the bar. Then you discover the menu: meat from the exceptional butcher Desnoyer, sea bass with a vegetable garnish, line-caught black sea bream or asparagus from Le Blayais. There is an impeccable selection of wines put together by Arnaud Bradol, the young owner. It's very difficult to decide between the *soupe de pêches* and the pear *clafoutis*. They like quality products here, and it shows.

— www.lesfinesgueules.fr

↑ **Les Fines Gueules** 2 rue la Vrilliere, Paris Ier – P. +33 1 42 61 35 41

LE FORUM

Why on earth is this so good? The spirits come in all colours with the most fashionable labels. There are more than 25 cocktail recipes and a third-millennium London ambience. The cocktails in this institution of Parisian nightlife, stirred not shaken by Josaine Biolatto, are true culinary concoctions. They radiate quality, inventiveness and humour. You could wile the night away just enjoying them.

— www.bar-le-forum.com

↑ **Le Forum** 4 boulevard Malesherbes, Paris VIIIᵉ – P. +33 1 42 65 37 86

FRENCHIE 🍴

"I went abroad at a very young age. I worked in New York and London. From what I learned during those years of training, I've tried to retain a spontaneous and honest way of cooking, and to use flavours that are considered unusual in France: pickles, chutneys and citrus condiments. As I work alone in the kitchen, I have to get down to the essentials, to the flavour. Afterwards, for the garnish, you know there is a French school of classical garden... I'm more the English garden type: I go for an organised chaos, but one that's always harmonious!" *Grégory Marchand*

— www.frenchie-restaurant.com

↑ **Frenchie** 5-6 rue du Nil, Paris IIe – P. +33 1 40 39 96 19

HARRY'S NEW YORK BAR

It's in the crowded red velour basement, on the very same piano that Gershwin composed 'An American in Paris'. The partitioning was burnt during the war, to light the stove. Americans in Paris still come here to delight in the legendary Irish coffee. Vibrant evenings are held here when the American presidential elections are drawing near.

 — www.harrysbar.fr

→ **Harry's New York Bar** 5 rue Daunou, Paris IIᵉ – P. +33 1 42 61 71 14

JEAN-PAUL HÉVIN CHOCOLATIER

Jean-Paul Hévin's chocolates are unique. His extra-dark chocolate cream fillings, Grand Cru beans, and not overly sweet creations could make you fear a slightly dry approach. But this doesn't emanate from coolness. It's elegance. He plays on chocolate-cheese-herb and spice combinations, such as Époisses cheesecumin, Pont-l'Évêque with thyme, goat's cheese-hazelnut and Roquefort-nut. Pure fine art.

— www.jeanpaulhevin.com

↑ **Jean-Paul Hévin chocolatier** 231 rue Saint-Honoré, Paris Iᵉʳ
P. +33 1 55 35 35 96

Suggestions

x Pizza **Alla Sarde** 22€ : fond Pissaladière, lit de Roquette, sardines en filets marinées à la vénitienne.

x Pizza **Stromboli** 26€ : fond Comté et saumuré de fenouil, sardines en filets marinées à la venitienne et écorces d'oranges confites, baie Rose.

x Pizza **torino** 22€ : fond mascarpone et gorgonzola, lit de pomme fruit, Roquette, jambon de Parme

x Pizza **trieste** 17€ : sauce tomate, Mozzarella, Roquette, jambon de Parme, copeaux de parmesan,

x Pizza **Capri** 15€ : huile d'olive, parmesan, Mozzarella, Ricotta et Epinard.

. Dessert 4.90€ : Coupe de fraise, chantilly aux Agrumes (maison)

IL CAMPIONISSIMO

"We could spend two months in search of the perfect balance of colour, crunchiness and softness for a pizza - sheer perfection! On top of that, our thing is the cooked and the raw. We often add raw ingredients to the pizza as soon as it comes out of the oven to add freshness, without spoiling the flavour. When I go into my lab to make a dough, I come out six hours later. I am constantly in search of the perfect recipe. Even my wife tells me to stop, but our guests are happy, and that's my aim..." *Gino Jaskula Toniolo*

 — www.ilcampionissimo.fr

↑ Il campionissimo 26 rue Leopold Bellan, Paris IIᵉ – P. +33 1 42 36 40 28

ĶEI

Kei Kobayashi is a very Japanese chef who is actually French! His influences are therefore mixed: the aestheticism, the verticality of his constructions, poetic harmony of colours and delicate flavours are inspired by Japan; while France has taught him the precision of actions and cooking times, meticulous finishing touches and respect for ingredients. The result is a rich and creative palette of subtle combinations where defined flavours culminate in a unique and perfectly executed cuisine.

— www.restaurant-kei.fr

➔ **Kei** 5 rue Coq-Héron, Paris Ier – P. +33 1 42 33 14 74

LE MEURICE - ALAIN DUCASSE

"Here I wanted to go back to basics, to start afresh with real flavours and original aromas and to let them express their own strength and subtlety. I wanted to give technique its true and only role, which is to reveal natural flavour. It's a radical approach - daring to create a cuisine that is unrefined in the sense that it works well precisely because of its simplicity. Complex preparation is pared away to leave strength of flavour at centre stage. This is the simple, true and complete story that I've been endeavouring to tell since I started in this profession and is the essence of what I'm doing today, aided by Christophe Saintagne." *Alain Ducasse*

— www.dorchestercollection.com

RACINES

Formerly from L'Arpège, Restaurant Laurent and Le Divellec, Nicolas Gauduin prepares his produce with talent and simplicity, under the watchful eye of owner David Lanher, a man with exacting standards. Fattened chickens and ducks, completely plucked, cooked whole in their skin, accompanied by fabulous crunchy seasonal vegetables from Alain Passard's kitchen garden. There is also a good selection of 'natural' wines, now also including other varieties.

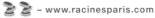 – www.racinesparis.com

↑ **Racines**   8 passage des Panoramas, Paris IIe – P. +33 1 40 13 06 41

OPÉRA - LOUVRE

77

PARIS

TERROIRS D'AVENIR

Across the street from the very hip and always packed Frenchie, Alexandre Drouard and Samuel Nahon's grocery is beginning to be noticed. This comes as no surprise when you find out that behind the sombre façade in light wood, these two dynamic and good-natured thirty-something-year-olds now offer the public the very best regional products, which until now were reserved exclusively for restaurateurs. Heirloom vegetables, these days only rarely grown, are once again being made accessible to consumers craving the real thing. Red cabbage, fresh horseradish and *scorzonera* arouse one's curiosity and desire to rediscover the flavours of days gone by.

↑ **Terroirs d'avenir – Grocery** 7 rue du Nil, Paris IIe – P. +33 1 45 08 48 80

TERROIRS D'AVENIR

One and the same sign conceals the fact that
there are in fact three shops here... As the
grocery was not enough to satisfy Alexandre
and Samuel's ambitions, they opened a fish
shop and a butcher's across the street. This
was enough to enable them to offer exceptional
meat and fish in addition to seasonal vegetables, always in keeping with their original
idea of supplying natural products directly
from small French producers. This great ini-
tiative is gaining momentum, from which we
can only benefit.

↑ **Terroirs d'avenir – Fish Monger/Butcher** 6 and 8 rue du Nil, Paris IIe

P. +33 1 45 08 48 80

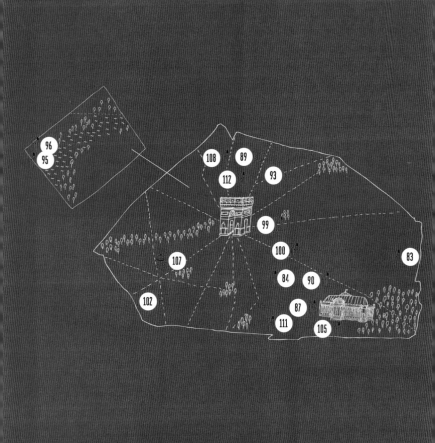

CHAMPS ÉLYSÉES

-

ÉTOILE

1728

Lafayette lived in this house and Madame de Pompadour held court here. The Asian-inspired cuisine served in the small and adorably quaint Trois Ors room is somewhat unusual but refreshingly different. More classic is the elegant tea menu, with pastries by Arnaud Larher, a disciple of Pierre Hermé.

 — www.restaurant-1728.com

↑ 1728   8 rue d'Anjou, Paris VIIIᵉ – P. +33 1 40 17 04 77

39 V

"Above all, 39V is a wonderful story of harmony. I wanted to gather together in this place the ingredients to make my recipe for happiness: love, involvement, humanity, good humour, conversation, sharing, discipline, beauty, sensuality, respect... and to put hospitality back into the heart of our daily preoccupations, both in the dining room and the kitchen. Located at the centre of the triangle d'or and hidden away under the rooftops of Paris, 39V is a haven of peace that offers genuine and simple cuisine." *Frédéric Vardon*

↑ 39 V   39 avenue George V, Paris VIIIᵉ – P. +33 1 56 62 39 05

ALAIN DUCASSE AU PLAZA ATHÉNÉE

With the reopening of the Plaza Athénée in the summer of 2014, Alain Ducasse is showcasing in his restaurant his new, very personal expression of contemporary French haute cuisine against the backdrop of a new décor by Patrick Jouin. The pillars of this cuisine are a trio of exceptional products - fish, vegetables, grains - prepared in a unique way. Patrons are not only invited to discover a dining experience: a one-of-a-kind event is in store for them.

 — www.dorchestercollection.com

↑ **Alain Ducasse au Plaza Athénée** 25 avenue Montaigne, Paris VIIIᵉ
P. +33 1 53 67 65 00

FROMAGERIE ALLEOSSE

Under the shop there is a cellar; actually, there are four cellars, one each for storing bloomy rind cheese, washed rind cheese, goat's cheese and tomme cheeses. This establishment is unique in Paris, as is the know-how of its master cheesemaker. There is a host of specialities from everywhere, with a preference for goat's cheese and extra-fresh burrata at weekends.

 — www.fromage-alleosse.com

↑ **Fromagerie Alleosse** 13 rue Poncelet, Paris XVIIe – P. +33 1 46 22 50 45

AUBRAC CORNER

'From farm to fork' is the fate of Christian Vallette's 320 cows. He makes them into hamburgers in his kitchen. Wait! Don't stop reading yet! This juicy and firm meat from Aubrac is mixed with wholegrain mustard mayonnaise. The bun, made from a combination of wheat and linseed, is as soft as white bread but with less sugar. There is just enough time for it to absorb the meat juices as you bite into the filling. You don't even need fries...

— www.maison-aubrac.com/aubrac-corner

→ Aubrac Corner 37 rue Marbeuf, Paris VIIIᵉ – P. +33 1 45 61 45 35

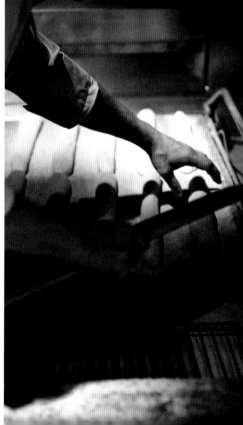

Sandwich Basque

Ciabatta thon

BE

Just because you lead a hectic life doesn't mean you have to eat badly. The bread here is made from scratch and baked in the oven that is the central fixture of this bakery-cum-grocery store. The sandwiches are made with the best fillings: tuna belly, sardines in oil, tomato confit, cured ham and rocket, among others. In five minutes your be box® is ready to take away. For your evening meal, have a blood sausage, a packet of good pasta and olive oil, which you'll find on the shelves. Just follow the instructions on the label. You will also find superb pastries and chocolate pizza.

 — www.boulangepicier.com

↑ BE 73 boulevard de Courcelles, Paris VIIIᵉ – P. +33 1 46 22 20 20

BOIS DE BOULOGNE : L'AUBERGE DU BONHEUR

Tucked away behind La Grande Cascade, and owned by the Menut family, is a tranquil place graced by nature in the heart of the city; a place with beautiful trees, gravel that crunches under your heels and garden furniture... Under the starlit sky, the tantalising aroma of grilled meat fills the air as it wafts from the kitchen. It's summer in Paris.

— www.restaurantsparisiens.com/restaurant-l-auberge-du-bonheur

↑ Bois de Boulogne : L'auberge du Bonheur Allée de Longchamp, Bois de Boulogne, Paris XVIᵉ – P. +33 1 42 24 10 17

BOIS DE BOULOGNE :
LA GRANDE CASCADE

At midday, you are charmed by the décor, the Second Empire pavilion and the cool murmuring of the waterfall. At night, away from Paris and the notion of time, you enjoy the elegant cuisine at this, the Menut family's flagship restaurant. Here the classics are treated with a good dose of inventiveness: escargots with verbena butter, baked cod steak with butternut mousseline or horseradish *espuma* and toasted *kouglof* to go with duck foie gras. As impressionist as a Sunday in the country.

 — www.restaurantsparisiens.com/restaurant-la-grande-cascade

↑ **Bois de Boulogne : La Grande Cascade** Allée de Longchamp, Bois de Boulogne, Paris XVIe – P. +33 1 45 27 33 51

CITRUS ÉTOILE

During his ten years in Hollywood, Gilles Epié learned the lessons of lively and light cuisine. Steaming and lemon juice are enough to bring out the best in food: duck foie gras ravioli with truffles and morels or steamed calf's liver with chanterelle mushrooms. The chic décor features a palette of electrifying citrus colours. Epié's wife Élizabeth, a former model he met in Los Angeles, supervises the front of house with enthusiasm and energy. She offers an extremely warm welcome to all guests.

 — www.citrusetoile.com

↑ **Citrus Étoile** 6 rue Arsène Houssaye, Paris VIIIe – P. +33 1 42 89 15 51

FOUQUET'S

There are celebrities in the room, and on the plates, too. The Merlan Colbert whiting is done in the style preferred by Robert Hossein; and there is Lobster Jean Todt and a palet au chocolat in honour of the César Awards. For those worried about their health but not wanting to miss out on a taste experience, dietician Paule Neyrat helped to create a tuna ceviche with starfruit juice and a monkfish stew with coconut and tamarind.

 — www.lucienbarriere.com/fr/hotel-luxe/Paris-Hotel-Fouquets-Barriere/Le-Fouquets.html

↑ **Fouquet's** 99 avenue des Champs-Elysées, Paris VIIIe – P. +33 1 40 69 60 50

BOULANGERIE FRÉDÉRIC LALOS

Exquisitely plump and golden brioches, bread with a perfectly crisp and brown crust, piles of Viennese pastries - each more appealing than the last - and baguettes with an elegance exclusively Parisian ... This place could only belong to Frédéric Lalos, winner of the Meilleur Ouvrier de France professional award and whose love for bread knows no bounds. In this sparsely decorated bakery in the rue de Belles-Feuilles, your eyes are drawn inexorably to the goods on display, with their wonderful aroma such as only tradition and skill can impart. But there is so much choice that, in the end, it's difficult to know where to look. The best thing is coming back for more.

Pain aux

↑ **Boulangerie Frédéric Lalos** 22 rue des Belles Feuilles, Paris XVIe
P. +33 1 47 27 48 17

LASSERRE

After the war, the modest bistro he founded moved into the adjacent mansion, which had been restored. This legendary restaurant is the fruit of the labours and passion of this man. Over the years, it earned him international renown and breathed life into a classic, delicate French cuisine. Today, Restaurant Lasserre has taken on a new impetus with the arrival of Christophe Moret. The opportunity was also taken to refresh the décor of the main dining room, where the retractable roof opens for dinner under the stars.

 — **www.restaurant-lasserre.com**

↑ **Lasserre** 17 avenue Franklin Delano Roosevelt, Paris VIIIᵉ – P. +33 1 43 59 02 13

LENÔTRE

Gaston Lenôtre, a true leading chef of his generation and creative genius, knew how to break the traditional mould of patisserie making. Over 40 years ago, this tasteful ambassador opened the first school for gastronomic training and improvement in France. Today, his know-how is upheld by the Lenôtre house, which continues to promote the French culinary heritage.

 — www.lenotre.com

↑ Lenôtre 48 avenue Victor Hugo, Paris XVIᵉ – P. +33 1 45 02 21 21

RECH

You open the door and sense the richness of the Atlantic coast. Soft lighting and pale wood reveal the refined touches exemplified by the damask tablecloths and agate butter dishes. And when the sole meunière for two arrives, coppery on the outside and soft and silky on the palate, even the seagulls are silent. Under the creative leadership of Jacques Maximin, the menu changes with the tides. Julien Dumas prepares nothing but the freshest and most splendid products from the sea and rivers.

 — www.restaurant-rech.fr

➜ **Rech** 62 avenue des Ternes, Paris XVIIe – P. +33 1 58 00 22 13

LE RELAIS PLAZA

Imagine the sophisticated dining room of the ocean liner the SS Normandie turned upside down by the heady madness of the Roaring Twenties. The Relais Plaza is just that: the height of elegance and exuberance. The cuisine in Philippe Marc's brasserie brings together Wiener schnitzel, steak tartare with matchstick potatoes and skewered veal sweetbreads, sometimes venturing into green lasagne with mascarpone and chanterelle mushrooms or crayfish in roast juices. A rum baba brings the cruise to an end beautifully.

 — www.dorchestercollection.com

↑ **Le Relais Plaza**   25 avenue Montaigne, Paris VIIIe – P. +33 1 53 67 66 02

RESTAURANT GUY SAVOY

"If I hadn't been born in France, I wouldn't have considered becoming a chef! And as for Paris, discovering its monuments, museums and perspectives has been a source of fascination for me. Paris is a theatre, where I've been happy to perform for years; my dishes are my stage and my ingredients are my script. As of the end of 2011, I'll be acting out my role at the Hôtel de la Monnaie, a magnificent building on the Quai de Conti, which has been an integral part of the landscape of the Seine and the Louvre since 1775." *Guy Savoy*

— www.guysavoy.com

↑ **Restaurant Guy Savoy** 18 rue Troyon, Paris XVIIe – P. +33 1 43 80 40 61

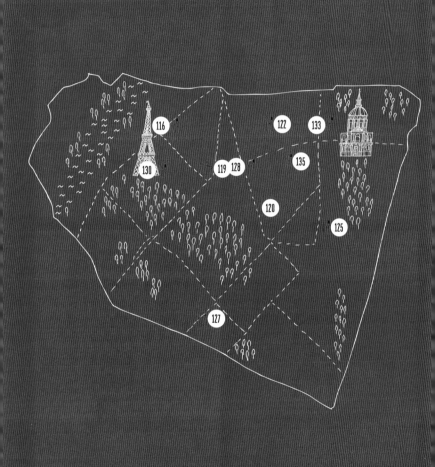

CHAMP DE MARS

—

INVALIDES

BATEAUX PARISIENS

You can hire one of these restaurant boats to take you down the Seine at twilight, or to enjoy any of their 'Prestige', 'Champagne', 'Jazz', 'Étoile' or 'Saveur' options for an intimate dinner. As the monuments begin to light up, the breeze is blowing and the imagination takes over. Green and white velouté cappuccino, duck breast in Port wine jus and iconic crêpes Suzette with orange butter bring out the magic of a supper under the lights. The extensive wine list is excellent. Whether you are from Paris or Tokyo, you will enjoy a special moment.

 — www.bateauxparisiens.com

↑ **Bateaux Parisiens**   Port de La Bourdonnais, Paris VIIe – P. +33 8 25 01 01 01

CAFÉ CONSTANT

Christian Constant has entrusted the reins of this establishment to the former head chef of his Les Fables de La Fontaine restaurant. The brasserie food is inspired by Constant's mother and revisited by one who knows what he's doing. You are transported back to his childhood with roast berry chicken within herb butter and vanilla rice pudding. There are also forays into more modern dishes such as saddle of rabbit ballotine with artichoke carpaccio, or crisp pastry-wrapped shrimp with basil. Come back the next morning for a chocolate croissant at the bar.

 — www.cafeconstant.com

FROMAGERIE MARIE-ANNE CANTIN

Daughter of Christian Cantin, founder of the Cheesemakers' Guild, Marie-Anne runs this business with her daughter and her husband Antoine. Holder of the Meilleur Ouvrier de France award, she is leading the fight against the standardisation of taste. Her cheeses are carefully chosen, having been produced in limited quantities by small-scale operations. Marie-Anne matures them in her own cellar, for several months in the case of the Beaufort and Comté cheeses. If you're passionate about cheese, you can arrange a tasting, which will be tailored to suit your palate.

— www.cantin.fr

CANTIN
fromages de tradition
AFFINEUR

➜ Fromagerie Marie-Anne Cantin 12 rue du Champs de Mars, Paris VIIe
P. +33 1 45 50 43 94

CHEZ L'AMI JEAN

"The philosophy behind my kitchen and cooking is simple: no partitions; no barriers; inspiration from tradition; being free... do you know what I mean? In fact just cooking! My strategy is to find the best produce, sourced from all over France, and then to do everything from A to Z, something different every day. Today I've made this: octopus terrine with foie gras and smoked salt. That's for today, but I don't know about tomorrow. The easy thing would be to make it again, but that wouldn't be any fun... Freedom is what counts here!" *Stéphane Jego*

 — www.lamijean.fr

↑ **Chez l'Ami Jean**   27 rue Malar, Paris VIIe – P. +33 1 47 05 86 89

PROTECTION DES MINEUR
ET
RÉPRESSION DE L'IVRESSE PUBLIQ

AUBERGE D'CHEZ EUX

Tableside carving? That is rare! The duck is served this way with its fig or pear accompaniment, depending on the season. Laurent and Catherine Brenta, from L'Évasion, manage this restaurant with its feel of the France of bygone days. Under the 1950 brine tub, diners attack the sausages, the starters trolley, the legendary cassoulet and the outstanding calf's head, but they surrender to the Paris-Brest.

— www.chezeux.com

↑ **Auberge d'chez eux** 2 avenue Lowendal, Paris VIIe – P. +33 1 47 05 52 55

ÉPICERIE DU PÈRE CLAUDE

Alain Ducasse: What boneless ham is this?

Ludovic Perraudin: 'Prince de Paris' - it's a ham from Brittany made in the traditional way. It isn't treated or chopped; the brine is injected into the ham, which is then rubbed in coarse salt. Only 250 hams are made this way each week, free from colouring, preservatives or gelatine.

AD: It has a fine, silky texture. Excellent. And it also smells like real ham. It's so unusual.

LP: How about a pickle?

AD: Of course not! That would ruin it.

 — www.epiceriedupereclaude.com

↑ **Épicerie du Père Claude** 4 rue du Général de Castelnau, Paris XVᵉ
P. +33 1 47 34 04 04

LA FONTAINE DE MARS

In this traditional bistro - complete with checked tablecloths, moleskin banquettes and straw-bottom chairs - Christiane and Jacques Boudon showcase products from the south-west of France: cassoulet with Tarbes beans, Basque country blood sausage by Christian Parra and tourtière landaise prune pie, among others. However they don't neglect the rest of the country, with their charcuterie products coming from Mainon Laborie in the Auvergne region, and Duval andouillette sausages. The eggs poached in Madiran wine are a highlight.

 — www.fontainedemars.com

↑ **La Fontaine de Mars**   129 rue Saint-Dominique, Paris Paris VIIe – P. +33 1 47 05 46 44

LE JULES VERNE

The Eiffel Tower - no Parisian can ever be indifferent about it. When it starts to sparkle the moment you look at it, and when you discover the lights of the city through the bay window, the Eiffel Tower offers you the magic of Paris as a gift. In this unique place, and iconic landmark of France, the cuisine Pascal Féraud serves is 100 per cent French. From olive oil to morel mushrooms, it is a tricolour rainbow of the best products from the country's regions. Down-to-earth cooking to accompany a moment of weightlessness.

 — www.lejulesverne-paris.com

↑ Le Jules Verne Tour Eiffel, avenue Gustave Eiffel, Paris VIIe – P. +33 1 45 55 61 44

PETROSSIAN

Armen Petrossian watches over his little pearls. He has brought his famous pressed caviar back into fashion. This skilful blend of beluga, osetra and sevruga caviars had once fallen into obscurity. But Petrossian isn't only about caviar. A royal Kamchatka crab leg reaches out to visitors. The fine flesh comes off like that of a lobster. The delicate aromas are almost sweet. Your palate wants to enjoy the pleasure of its wondrously light texture to very the last morsel. This is crab at its finest.

— www.petrossian.fr

↑ **Petrossian**   18 boulevard de la Tour-Maubourg, Paris VIIe – P. +33 1 44 11 32 22

79 rue Saint-Dominique, Paris VIIe – P. +33 1 47 05 49 75

↑ Hôtel Thoumieux

HÔTEL THOUMIEUX

Jean-François Piège has, together with Thierry Costes, taken over this hotel in the 7th arrondissement. The menu of the new Thoumieux has two parts: 'Room Service' for classic dishes such as squid carbonara and *lièvre* (hare) *à la royale*; and 'Ma Cuisine' for the chef's more audacious offerings, such as live langoustines with coconut and puffed pizza with tuna and rocket. The desserts are exquisite. Upstairs there is a small dining room for exclusive cuisine, and ten hotel rooms.

 — www.thoumieux.fr

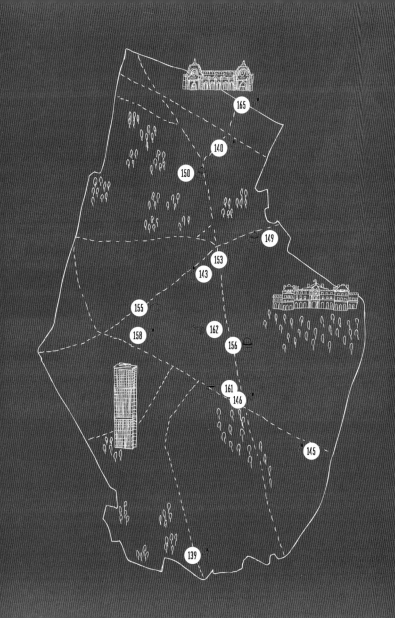

MONTPARNASSE

–

LUXEMBOURG

L'ASSIETTE

Alain Ducasse: What are you going to let us try today?

David Rathgeber: My sauté gourmand: veal sweetbreads, crayfish, wild mushrooms and warm foie gras. I do large sweetbread escalopes in a beurre mousseux. I add the crayfish, the Saint George's mushrooms and a few asparagus tips. Then I deglaze with cognac. I cover lightly with the Nantua sauce before adding the foie gras escalopes, the *fleur de sel* and a good sprinkling of pepper... *À table!*

 — www.restaurant-lassiette.com

→ **L'Assiette** 181 rue du Château, Paris XIVe — P. +33 1 43 22 64 86

L'ATELIER DE JOËL ROBUCHON

"When Robuchon wanted to create a new restaurant concept in 2003, he naturally joined forces with his main associates. We didn't want to work under pressure, and, above all, we wanted to be physically closer to our patrons, which is why we have this open kitchen. The way the kitchen works has also evolved. We always use quality produce, reared or harvested directly by our suppliers, and prepared with great simplicity. Today we welcome our guests as friends; it's our finest reward." *Éric Lecerf*

— www.joel-robuchon.com

→ **L'Atelier de Joël Robuchon** 5 rue de Montalembert, Paris VIIe
P. +33 1 42 22 56 56

LE CHERCHE MIDI

The antipasti of the house, fish of the day and carpaccios are of unquestionable freshness. They go hand in hand with remarkable olive oil and very good mozzarella. No pizzas, nor any combination of unusual products, just the produce prepared in a traditional way, with simplicity. You'll find a warm atmosphere in the small, tightly packed room, as well as a terrace, which is chock-full in good weather.

 — www.lecherchemidi.fr

↑ **Le Cherche Midi** 22 rue du Cherche Midi, Paris VIᵉ – P. +33 1 45 48 27 44

LA CLOSERIE DES LILAS

You automatically look under the banquette in case Picasso left behind a splash of paint, Hemingway a page of one of his manuscripts or Rimbaud a free verse. Regulars who come here - even in Aragon's day - are in the know: you have to go to the brasserie, the restaurant is for the bourgeois. What matters is that you enjoy the arbour and its famous lilac trees, while letting the legendary hand-cut steak tartare or haddock à la crème melt in your mouth and tantalise your tastebuds.

— www.closeriedeslilas.fr

↑ La Closerie des Lilas 171 boulevard du Montparnasse, Paris VIe
P. +33 1 40 51 34 50

LE DÔME

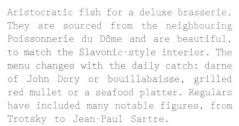

Aristocratic fish for a deluxe brasserie. They are sourced from the neighbouring Poissonnerie du Dôme and are beautiful, to match the Slavonic-style interior. The menu changes with the daily catch: darne of John Dory or bouillabaisse, grilled red mullet or a seafood platter. Regulars have included many notable figures, from Trotsky to Jean-Paul Sartre.

↑ **Le Dôme** 108 boulevard du Montparnasse, Paris XIVe – P. +33 1 43 35 25 81

PIERRE HERMÉ PARIS

Pierre Hermé: So, would you like to taste a macaroon? This one is jasmine-flavoured. There's also cinnamon-cherry-pistachio, rose, chocolate, caramel, wasabi-strawberry, apricot-pistachio and milk chocolate passionfruit, among many others...

Alain Ducasse: You know that I like them hard, without fillings!

PH: Personally, I like them soft, creamy, smooth as can be, with just a light crunchy crust. There are many different palates!

 — www.pierreherme.com

↑ **Pierre Hermé Paris**   72 rue Bonaparte, Paris VIᵉ – P. +33 1 43 54 47 77

LA PÂTISSERIE DES RÊVES

A *millefeuille*, theoretically, is crispy. On the other hand, it's not. This one melts in your mouth. It fades away like an aristocrat, in a rustle of vanilla-flavoured cream, which lasts until the last puff, thanks to the pastry chef's unrelenting technique in corsetry. Only on Sundays, otherwise people would no longer go to work. Following the rue du Bac, Philippe Conticini, one of the greatest pastry chefs of his generation, invested in rue de Longchamp. Finally!`

 — www.lapatisseriedesreves.com

↑ **La Pâtisserie des Rêves** 93 rue du Bac, Paris VIIe – P. +33 1 42 84 00 82

BOULANGERIE POILANE

Apollonia Poilâne: The iconic Parisian baguette is white bread, originally for the rich. Our establishment became successful when people migrated from the provinces and wanted *pain paysan*, country-style bread with rye.

Alain Ducasse: To eat with their rillettes, ham and sausage...

AP: Exactly. And the canvases you can see above me are by starving painters from the district who would trade their works for a loaf of bread. '*Une croûte contre une croûte*' ('a bad painting for a crust of bread') is what they would say.

 — www.poilane.fr

↑ Boulangerie Poilane 8 rue du Cherche-Midi, Paris VIe – P. +33 1 45 48 42 59

153 MONTPARNASSE · LUXEMBOURG PARIS

FROMAGERIE QUATREHOMME

In the business for 25 years, Marie Quatrehomme, Meilleur Ouvrier de France awarded, manages three Parisian boutiques. She also supplies the hotel Le Meurice, Pierre Gagnaiire and Guy Savoy. We are well aware, too, that as early as 20 years ago the team had no qualms in unveiling Roquefort Carles, less popular, less expensive and less salty than its well-known rivals. The range of refined cheeses satisfies almost every palate.

 — **www.quatrehomme.fr**

↑ Fromagerie Quatrehomme   62 rue de Sèvres, Paris VIIe – P. +33 1 47 34 33 45

MARCHÉ RASPAIL

A market that offers three full meals: the all-day menu stretches the length of Boulevard Raspail. For breakfast: English muffins, home-baked with a smile, and poached eggs. At lunch, it's very tempting to send the entire array of organic vegetables to the roasting pan. And for dinner, roast suckling pig, very good farm cheeses, citrus salad. If we could, we'd cook this way all year round.

→ **Marché Raspail** Boulevard Raspail, Paris VIe

RESTAURANT JOSÉPHINE

Come on! There's still a little room for a generous serving of *millefeuille* or the divine Grand Marnier soufflé... A guarantee of tradition, this is a family business that has been handed down to the next generation. With its worn leather and the patina on the silver, patterned mirrors and home cooking, 'Chez Dumonet' as the locals know it, is an authentic 1920s Parisian bistro. The terrines and foie gras are homemade and the steak tartare is prepared in the dining room. All is as it should be. Largesse is on the menu at Chez Dumonet; it's a matter of principle.

↑ **Restaurant Joséphine** Chez Dumonet, 117 rue du Cherche-Midi, Paris VIe
P. +33 1 45 48 52 40

LE SELECT

Two round and proud pots, one large and one small, find their way to your table. First comes the rich, heady melted dark chocolate. Then the caress of frothing milk. This is the traditional hot chocolate served at Le Select, thick as a plush pile woollen carpet and as comforting as a roaring fire. A little of the Dadaist soul of Montparnasse still lingers at the bottom of the pot.

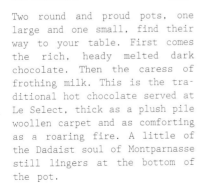

↑ **Le Select** 99 boulevard du Montparnasse, Paris VIᵉ – P. +33 1 45 44 56 45

GILLES VÉROT – CHARCUTIER

Champion of France for his brawn; an award for best liver pâté – the list goes on: Gilles Vérot is doing justice to his pigs. We really like his ham pasties and his pistachio meat pie intended 'for the purists'. Excellent quality of parsley-garnished jellied hams and sausages. A very good pork butcher – just the way we like them – who is also winning over New Yorkers with Daniel Boulud.

 — www.verot-charcuterie.fr

↑ **Gilles Vérot – Charcutier** 3 rue Notre-Dame des Champs, Paris VIᵉ
P. +33 1 45 48 83 32

LE VOLTAIRE

An egg is cut in half. Then things become complicated. A few slices of radish, a small bunch of green beans and sliced fresh button mushrooms. Followed by a beautiful mayonnaise made with cream and mustard, coating the eggs with a new shell. A sprig of chervil forms an exclamation mark between two tomato smiles. This is how we like our egg with mayonnaise.

↑ **Le Voltaire** 27 Quai Voltaire, Paris VIIᵉ – P. +33 1 42 61 17 49

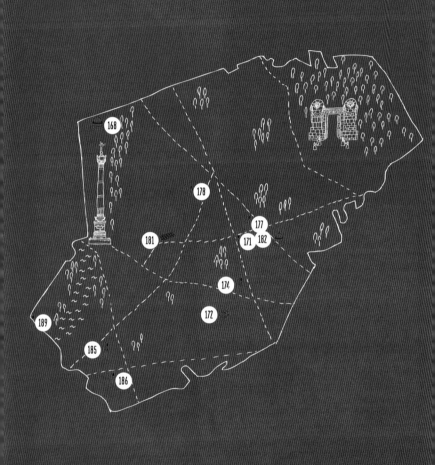

BASTILLE

–

BELLEVILLE

MARCHÉ BASTILLE

This is one of the largest markets in Paris, bringing together around a hundred stallholders. You are spoilt for choice with such reasonable prices. The products sold here are often of good quality, like the fish at the stall run by Jacky Lorenzo, a popular figure at the market. Tourists come to admire the regional produce, while we appreciate the lively atmosphere in this genuine neighbourhood market.

↑ **Marché Bastille** Boulevard Richard Lenoir, Paris XIᵉ

BISTROT PAUL BERT

Jean Gabin is having problems with his son, a lad named Claude Brasseur, and with his daughter, Jeanne Moreau. Gabin is from the country, Brasseur is a racing cyclist and Jeanne Moreau is infatuated with an old beau. When you sit down in Bistrot Paul Bert, what you see is Gas-oil (Hi-Jack Highway), Gabin's great films, Moreau's smile and Paris in black and white.

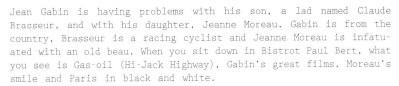

BOUCHERIE MICHEL BRUNON

The carcass swings along a rail as if in a train crash, an inch away from the pretty brunette who is making chipolatas. There is a roar of sirloins, ribs and legs. "This is a product for the initiated," laughs Michel Brunon with a perfectly aged rib steak in his hand. It can be cut with a fork. "I age all my meat myself, otherwise I won't eat it. And if I don't eat it, I won't sell it to my customers. I'm a butcher, not a meat seller."

↑ **Boucherie Michel Brunon** Marché Beauveau, place d'Aligre, Paris XIIe

P. +33 1 43 40 62 58

CAFFÈ DEI CIOPPI

Delicacy, your name is sbrisolona. A little dry biscuit that doesn't look like much, really, or maybe just like a biscuit! Powdered almonds, cornflour. Sink your teeth into it, though, and it's just like Verdi at La Scala, or a dive into the Trevi Fountain - in this case, into a little mascarpone cream pot. Fabrizio and Federica don't stop at the sweets, of course. They prepare pure, simple trattoria cuisine with great panache.

→ **Caffè Dei Cioppi** 159 rue du Faubourg Saint-Antoine, Paris XIᵉ
P. +33 1 43 46 10 14

LE CHARDENOUX

"I was looking for a very Parisian location, where I could create an easy and uncomplicated cuisine. A bistro is associated with the idea of a chef - timeless, charming, authentic, gourmet... I pushed open the door at Le Chardenoux and I said to myself: this is the place. We've been interpreting the great Parisian classics ever since: beef tartare, Landes asparagus with mimosa sauce, saddle of lamb cooked in a clay crust, chicken cooked in hay, French toast, waffles. But this doesn't mean we can't do other more exotic things, like curried clams, for instance." *Cyril Lignac*

 — www.restaurantlechardenoux.com

↑ **Le Chardenoux** 1 rue Jules Vallès, Paris XIe – P. +33 1 43 71 49 52

CHEZALINE

Not only has the retro-style décor of an old horse-butcher's shop been retained in this bijou delicatessen and bar, but Delphine Zampetti - formerly of Café Caché du 104 and Verre Volé - has also kept its soul. There is no horse meat here now, but there are excellent products with which to create gourmet sandwiches to order - the chicken *pot-au-feu* is to die for - or salads and daily specials and desserts. Ideal for a well-deserved break in the heart of the Bastille district.

→ **Chezaline** 85 rue de la Roquette, Paris XIe – P. +33 1 43 71 90 75

LE CHOCOLAT ALAIN DUCASSE – MANUFACTURE À PARIS

"Cross the paved courtyard and enter a chocolate-lover's paradise. Jute sacks filled with the best beans carefully selected from around the world, the sometimes deafening sound of machines - a roaster, sorter, winnow, crusher, concher... - brought here from all over Europe, the bitter and rich smell of raw chocolate, and the more sensual, sweet and varied aromas of individual chocolates and bars will draw you into a physical, sensory, sensual and epicurean world."
Alain Ducasse

 — www.lechocolat-alainducasse.com

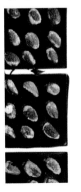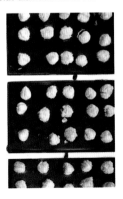

↑ **Le Chocolat Alain Ducasse – Manufacture à Paris**
40 rue de la Roquette, Paris XIe
P. +33 1 48 05 82 86

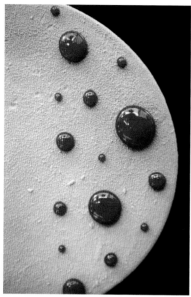

PÂTISSERIE CYRIL LIGNAC

In the delightful rue Paul Bert - one of the most deliciously enticing in Paris - Cyril Lignac, together with Benoît Couvrand, chose to open his first pâtisserie, with lovely clean lines, right across the street from his restaurant Chardenoux! Also a pastry chef by trade, Cyril Lignac entices us with his interpretation of the world of sweet things: a solid traditional base, a style suffused with chic originality and, above all, abundant talent. This is the secret behind the success of his lemon meringue pie, Paris-Brest and baba with vanilla Chantilly cream, but also his bread, pastries and other sweet treats...

— www.lapatisseriecyrillignac.com

BASTILLE - BELLEVILLE

183

PARIS

↑ Pâtisserie Cyril Lignac 24 rue Paul Bert, Paris XIe – P. +33 1 43 72 74 88

LE QUINCY

Come rain, hail or shine, you'll find a bow tie on the menu. Appearing just above is Bobosse, the down-to-earth owner of a mountain inn right in the middle of Paris. Enormous plates, fresh produce, French recipes. It's crayfish season, real 'red claws'. As the innkeeper would say: "You just have to peel them apart for yourself"!

— www.lequincy.fr

↑ **Le Quincy** 28 avenue Ledru-Rollin, Paris XIIᵉ – P. +33 1 46 28 46 76

LE TRAIN BLEU

Stationary travellers set off for a realm of gilt and frescos. When studying the ceiling, their imaginations wander the Île de France, sleepily cross the Rhône and awake at the seaside. The trains are outside, and there is noise and bustle, with people arriving, departing and staying behind. On the table, in the shadow of the huge booths, a baba chantilly glows.

 — www.le-train-bleu.com

↑ **Le Train Bleu**   Gare de Lyon, place Louis Armand, Paris XIIᵉ – P. +33 1 43 43 09 06

YACHTS DE PARIS

We embark on the privately booked Cachemire for an intimate gourmet cruise. Guy Krenzler, holder of the Meilleur Ouvrier de France award, is in charge of the food. Citrus-marinated scallops, avocado in suzette sauce, foie gras confit, peppered grapes and walnuts and black truffle emulsion are served. There is Baccarat crystal glassware and a marble fireplace, all of which makes this the sophisticated way to appreciate Paris and the Seine.

— www.yachtsdeparis.fr/

BASTILLE - BELLEVILLE
189
PARIS

↑ **Yachts de Paris**   Port Henri IV, Paris IVᵉ – P. +33 1 44 54 14 70

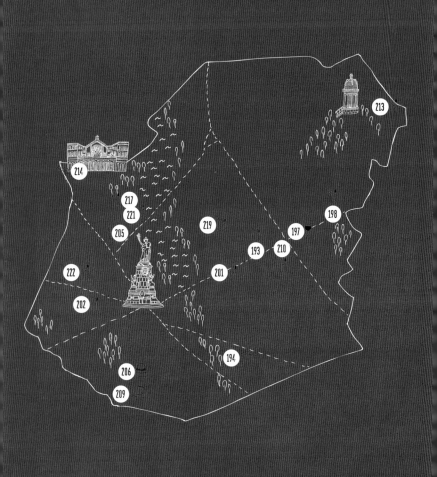

RÉPUBLIQUE

—

BUTTES CHAUMONT

ASIE ANTILLES AFRIQUE

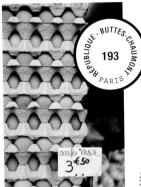

ASIE ANTILLES AFRIQUE

The whole world contained in a hessian bag. One slaloms between the mountains of rice from all continents and legumes, yams and sweet potatoes in a variety of colours. It's packed with African mamas and Chinese papas. A West Indian man has come to choose his pork in vinegar and his '*bonda Man Jacques*' or 'the behind of mother Jacques' peppers, in Creole. Fans of the exotic, and taste adventurers, leave with two different types of plantain bananas to sample.

↑ **Asie Antilles Afrique**   88 bis rue du Faubourg du Temple, Paris XIe

AUX DEUX AMIS

Aux Deux Amis has been rejuvenated. While the décor hasn't changed, the menu has been updated. Quench your thirst with a glass of *vin nature* before sitting under the neon lights to enjoy the daily specials. There is no need to make things complex for them to be good; just enjoy the moment. Don't forget to have your last drink outside on the terrace and take in the buzzing street atmosphere!

↑ Aux Deux Amis 45 rue Oberkampf, Paris XIe – P. +33 1 58 30 38 13

BAR AUX FOLIES 🍷

This place was once a cabaret where Piaf and Maurice Chevalier sang. It has retained the feel of a Parisian café théâtre with its columns and mosaic floor. You can have your coffee while standing at the counter like in the old days, avoiding the reflection of the coloured neon lights in the large mirror that runs along the bar. Or indulge in the pleasure of a beer on the terrace while watching the world stroll by. You'll suddenly feel completely at ease there, in the true Parisian spirit.

 — www.aux-folies-belleville.fr

↑ **Bar Aux Folies** 8 rue de Belleville, Paris XXᵉ — P. +33 6 14 17 91 33

LE BARATIN

Raquel doesn't speak. She has no time, because time is of the essence. Simplicity is simmering gently in the serenity of her large shiny aluminium pans and the intimacy of her tiny kitchen. The delicate monkfish liver terrine, mackerel sashimi, horseradish and fresh raspberries display the colours of her personal and perfectly disciplined cuisine. The list of *vins nature* chosen by Philippe Pinoteau, 'Pinuche' to his friends, are a real talking point, and will no doubt take care of conversation.

↑ **Le Baratin** 3 rue Jouye-Rouve, Paris XXᵉ – P. +33 1 43 49 39 70

LE CHATEAUBRIAND

Warning, cuisine on the move - frequent turbulence; chance of dizziness; unexpected encounters with shellfish and dashi; anchovies or mango coming aground on a carpaccio. At the helm, Inaki Aizpitarte smiles behind his beard. Drawing on his Basque roots, he creates a soft fruit piperade and a rose-flavoured fromage frais. For dessert, he is bold enough to serve his already famous *banane ecrasée* (mashed banana). You come back to land a little shaken after having discovered new horizons; it's as if you have just gone for a spin in a flying saucer.

 — www.lechateaubriand.net

↑ **Le Chateaubriand**   129 avenue Parmentier, Paris XIᵉ — P. +33 1 43 57 45 95

CHEZ L'AMI LOUIS

In 1924, this establishment, which served bouillon and fried dishes, was owned by Louis Pedebosq. Antoine Magnin bought the business in 1936 and continued to offer traditional cuisine. Several generations of customers frequent the restaurant today, each of whom has a particular emotional attachment to it. Its last owner, Thierry de La Brosse, perfectly preserved the spirit of the place. Now that he has joined the angels, it is certain that his successors will, under the benevolent supervision of Monsieur Louis, be able to carry on his legacy.

SANCERRE LES MONTS DAMNÉS 2008 D. BOURGEOIS 68 – TRONÇOY LALANDE 2005 81 –VIEUX CHATEAU LANDON 2005 60 – M.A VENT MERLIN 2005 56 – MARIUS 2005 125 – RESERVE DE LOUIS 2006 56

FOIE GRAS DES LANDES	57
JAMBON PATA NEGRA	52
CONFIT DE CANARD FROID	38
ESCARGOTS DE BOURGOGNE LA DZ	39
CUISSES DE GRENOUILLES A LA PROVENCALE	60

AGNEAU DE LAIT ROTI P. BEARNAISES 2 pers. 64 p. pers.
COTE DE BOEUF GRILLEE   2 pers. 60 p. pers.
ENTRECOTE   POELEE   64
COTES DE MOUTON GRILLEES 45
CONFIT DE CANARD AUX POMMES BEARNAISE 47
COTE DE VEAU GRILLEE 47
COTE DE VEAU A LA CREME 53
ROGNON DE VEAU GRILLE 48
ROGNON DE VEAU FLAMBE 54
PIGEON ROTI AUX PETITS POIS 49
CAILLES D ELEVAGE AUX RAISINS 45
POULET ROTI (entier) 78 2pers

                           SALADE

FRUITS DE SAISON
FRUITS ROUGES (selon arrivage) 24
GÂTEAU AU CHOCOLAT 24
NOUGATINE AU RHUM   24
ANANAS FRAIS 24 OU AU KIRSCH 24
PRUNEAUX A L ARMAGNAC 24
GLACES ET SORBETS AU CHOIX 24
              PRIX NETS SERVICE 15% COMPRIS

→ **Chez l'Ami Louis** 32 rue du Vertbois, Paris IIIe – P. +33 1 48 87 77 48

DU PAIN ET DES IDÉES

"Time makes the difference - time and the number of stages. Working slowly keeps the leavening wilder. But it's also more fragile. It's like wine. Certain types of leavening will express themselves if you aren't too aggressive with them. It's living beings that are transformed; you can only adapt to the material."

Christophe Vasseur, baker

 — www.dupainetdesidees.com

↑ **Du Pain et des Idées** 34 rue Yves Toudic, Paris Xe – P. +33 1 42 40 44 52

MARCHÉ DES ENFANTS ROUGES

The orphanage founded here by Queen Margot and the red uniforms of its occupants have given way to a neighbourhood market. When it opened in 1777, there was even a well and a cowshed. Today, the little market is housed in a glazed hall. It is like a village square and has the same charm. It's peaceful during the week, but bustling on Sundays. You can have a light snack at one of the stallholders' tables or in the pretty square surrounding the market.

↑ **Marché des Enfants Rouges** 39 rue de Bretagne, Paris IIIe

HÔTEL DU PETIT MOULIN

Outside is a bakery dating from 1900; inside, is a journey. There is something of Fellini in the red and lilac velvet which clashes with a leopard print cushion and a turquoise stool. There is music in these rooms, which either glitter at night like a Venetian mask or, on the contrary, are starkly rendered in a Provençal limewash. The moments you spend here, enclosed in this whimsical cocoon, are unique. The décor is by Christian Lacroix. It's up to you to find a costume...

 — www.hotelpetitmoulinparis.com

↑ **Hôtel du Petit Moulin** 29 rue de Poitou, Paris IIIe – P. +33 1 42 74 10 10

PHO DÔNG HUÔNG

The ideal would be to have a huge paper serviette for a more comfortable tasting experience. As soon as you're seated, the waiter brings a mysterious-looking brown and creamy sauce to the table, with a plate of extremely fresh herbs and spices. If you're a beginner, do what the person sitting next to you does - dip the crunchy soya bean sprouts in the sauce. As simple as that! Pho Dong Huong is a legendary family-run Vietnamese temple. Special mention goes to the frittered crêpe and the *bo bun cha gio*.

— www.dong-huong.com/accueil/

↑ **Pho Dông Huong** 14 rue Louis Bonnet, Paris XIᵉ – P. +33 1 43 38 25 74

ROSA BONHEUR 🍴

Here is a privileged spot for a terrace, laid out amid the trees in the heart of Buttes Chaumont Park. The Ibérico ham tapas, small salads and Basque pâté are perfect for a country-style brunch, perhaps taken on the lawn as a clandestine picnic with all of Paris at your feet. When the sun makes you feel as if you're in Spain, the mostly bio wines served on the terrace go perfectly with chorizo.

🐌 — www.rosabonheur.fr

↑ **Rosa Bonheur** 2 allée de la Cascade - Parc des Buttes-Chaumont, Paris XIXᵉ
P. +33 1 42 00 00 45

SCHMID TRAITEUR

When they say the whole of Alsace, they really mean the whole of Alsace. From horseradish to Black Forest cake, you pass through an ocean of cooked-meat cuts. There is turnip pickled in brine, which can be served just as you would sauerkraut, and both plain liver sausages and truffled ones that can be used as a spread. You can chew on a pretzel while awaiting your turn. It's Christmas under a cloud of icing sugar, and this has lasted for a full century.

 — www.schmid-traiteur.com

→ **Schmid Traiteur** 76 boulevard de Strasbourg, Paris Xe – P. +33 1 46 07 89 74

SOL SEMILLA

On the vegan Sunday brunch menu: blinis with almond purée and alfalfa bean sprouts, half-cooked, half-raw soup, banana-milk-rice-lacuma-maca milkshake, the traditional *xocolatl* of the Aztecs, with cinnamon. Pascal, a dietician and druid from time to time, willingly introduces 'superfoods'. At the same time, Jean-François goes to meet Parisians at the organic markets. You can shop there, eat on the premises and leave armed with the day's menu.

— www.sol-semilla.fr

↑ **Sol semilla** 23 rue des Vinaigriers, Paris X^e – P. +33 1 42 01 03 44

LA TÊTE DANS LES OLIVES

Cédric Casanova: So, chef, what are you going to make from my olives?

Alain Ducasse: Mamma mia, they're very salty! I'll start by soaking them for 48 hours in fresh water. Afterwards, I'll add olive oil - but which one?

CC: Preferably the Bianca one. It's light and refined, with lemon aromas. In the large tin cruet.

AD: Good idea. Pass me the fennel seeds, in the basket over there, and the pink pepper.

CC: *Buon appetito!*

 — www.latetedanslesolives.com

↑ La tête dans les olives   2 rue Sainte-Marthe, Paris Xᵉ – P. +33 9 51 31 33 34

LE VERRE VOLÉ

Alain Ducasse: So, what are we eating today?

Cyril Bordarier: A rib steak from Desnoyer, or sea bass that comes directly from an auction in the Channel. The cauliflower is Annie Bertin's. The capers come from La Tête dans les Olives and dessert is from Desmoulins, in Boulevard Voltaire. Do you want to try it?

AD: Of course.

CB: Enjoy, it's today's menu. It'll change tomorrow.

 — www.leverrevole.fr

↑ **Le Verre Volé** 67 rue Lancry, Paris X^e – P. +33 1 48 03 17 34

ZERDA CAFÉ

Jaffar Achour: Here is the vegetable Berber couscous. You must oil the semolina as soon as it comes out of the steam - burning your hands in the process - otherwise it becomes oily. It's a spring couscous. On the side are finely sliced, crunchy onions.

Alain Ducasse: In fact, there is a whole range of different types of couscous...

JA: As far as we know, almost 450... We also prepare *berkoukes*, with larger rolled grains. It's prepared with or without meat. Here, we also serve it with shellfish.

— www.zerdacafe.fr

PORTE DU MAROC

→ **Zerda Café** 15 rue René Boulanger, Paris X^e – P. +33 1 42 00 25 15

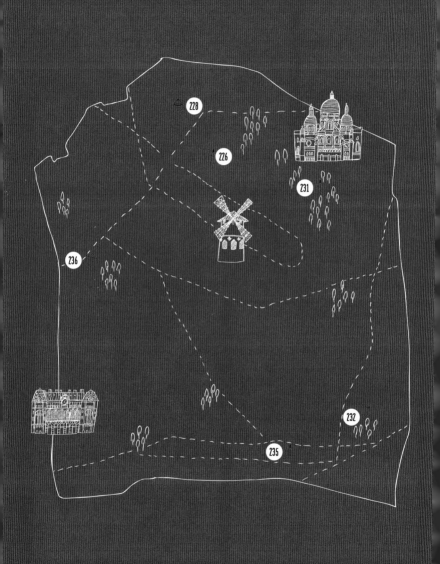

ROCHECHOUART
-
SACRÉ-COEUR

LE COQ RICO

This bistro opened by Antoine Westermann in 2012 pays tribute to the creatures of the farmyard. The Dombes duck confit is lavishly prepared, smoked magret is combined with roasted cod in a spectacular dish, while the supreme of yellow Gers chicken is concealed behind an almond and hazelnut crust that is to die for. As a starter, the terrines vie for attention with the fresh eggs cooked in a multitude of ways. The chicken is done in every way possible to bring out its best, and there is something here for everyone.

 — www.lecoqrico.com

↑ **Le Coq Rico** 98 rue Lepic, Paris Paris XVIIIe – P. +33 1 42 59 82 89

PÂTISSERIE ARNAUD LARHER

Trained at Fauchon and Pierre Hermé, this man did not wait for his tricolour stripe, achieved in 2007, to write his name in gold dust in the world of delicacies. His creations - such as his chocolate marshmallow or his 'Frisson', lime-pulp ganache - remain both in mouth and memory for a long time. Arnaud Larher creates a pink poppy éclair, and revisits the pistachio macaroon. Ices in summer; hot chocolate, old-style, in winter ends up drowning its taster in sinfulness. Too cute.

 — www.arnaud-larher.com

RÉPUBLIQUE · BUTTES-CHAUMONT

229

PARIS

→ Pâtisserie Arnaud Larher 53 rue Caulaincourt, Paris XVIIIᵉ – P. +33 1 42 57 68 08

MICHELANGELO

Every morning, under the shade of the Montmartre cable car, Michelangelo Riina, a straightforward Sicilian, goes to the market and composes the menu. Every evening, he - alone - paces up and down the few centimetres that separate the open kitchen from his 15 or so guests. Between his hands, Sicilian cuisine bursts with flavours and colours, like his Gorgonzola arancini. Imagination, too, such as his giant prawn and pistachio tagliatelle. A well-mastered and modern Mediterranean experience.

↑ **Michelangelo**   3 rue André Barsacq, Paris XVIIIᵉ – P. +33 1 42 23 10 77

PICCOLA TOSCANA

You push open the deli's door and, just like in Florence, you order a *tramezzino alla porchetta* - a roast suckling pig sandwich. While it's being prepared, immerse yourself in the refined pecorinos or the Margherita panforte, a Siennese nougat with candied citrus fruit. Let yourself be tempted by the communal table for dining guests and the little terrace for a plate of truffled pasta.

— www.piccola-toscana.com

↑ **Piccola Toscana**   10 rue Rochambeau, Paris IXᵉ – P. +33 9 51 04 46 35

POUSSE POUSSE 🍴

A whole-living-foods specialist, Lawrence Aboucaya owns a small deli-restaurant. Using sprouts, young shoots and wheatgrass, juice is made with a special extractor so as not to 'break up the molecules'. The same principle is applied to quiches, salads, vegetable or fresh fruit juices, all presented in an ornate, warm and cosy ambiance.

🌀 — www.poussepousse.eu

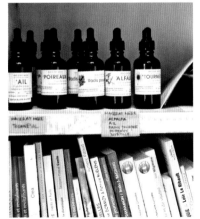

↑ **Pousse Pousse** 7 rue Notre-Dame de Lorette, Paris IXe – P. +33 1 53 16 10 81

WEPLER

What is there to see here? There's the atmosphere and the setting; this is a genuine Parisian brasserie. Everyone from Bonnard to Picasso, from Henry Miller to Blier and Truffaut, who filmed a scene from *Les Quatre Cent Coups* (The 400 Blows) here, were wild about the authenticity of the place. What is there to eat? Oysters - this establishment was the first to make them its speciality over a century ago - and *choucroute*, or Béarnaise grilled pig's trotters. It's authentic, we say.

 — www.wepler.com

→ Wepler 14 place Clichy, Paris XVIIIe – P. +33 1 45 22 53 29

ALPHABETICAL INDEX

INDEX BY AREA

242

CREDITS

COLLECTION DIRECTOR
Emmanuel Jirou-Najou

EDITORIAL MANAGER
Alice Gouget

PUBLISHER
Jessica Rostain

EDITORIAL DIRECTION
Aurore Charoy
Vianney Drouin

WRITER
Claire Dixsaut
Frédérick E. Grasser Hermé
Christophe Saintagne

PHOTOGRAPHY
Pierre Monetta

ART DIRECTION / GRAPHIC DESIGN
Pierre Tachon / Soins graphiques
Merci à Sophie Brice

PHOTO- ENGRAVING
Nord Compo

MARKETING AND COMMUNICATION
Camille Gonnet
camille.gonnet@alain-ducasse.com

This edition published in 2014
by Hardie Grant Books

Hardie Grant Books (Australia)
Ground Floor, Building 1
658 Church Street
Richmond, Victoria 3121
www.hardiegrant.com.au

Hardie Grant Books (UK)
5th & 6th Floor
52 54 Southwark Street
London SE1 1RU
www.hardiegrant.co.uk

All rights reserved. No part
of this publication may
be reproduced, stored in a
retrieval system or transmitted
in any form by any means,
electronic, mechanical,
photocopying, recording or
otherwise, without the prior
written permission of the
publishers and copyright
holders.

The moral rights of the author
have been asserted.

Printed in China
Legal Deposit : 4th quarter 2014
ISBN : 9781742708997

© ALAIN DUCASSE Édition 2014
84, avenue Victor Cresson
92130 Issy-les-Moulineaux

www.alain-ducasse.com

ALSO AVAILABLE FROM ALAIN DUCASSE

Featuring award-winning restaurants, classic food destinations, hidden gems and the best markets and suppliers, Alain Ducasse's comprehensive guides are invitations to discover the best culinary offerings of some of the most exciting cities around the world. Each book includes a removable full-colour guidebook.

RRP £35.00 / 450-600 pages / 252 x 189 mm

Available at all good booksellers or at
www.hardiegrant.co.uk